DON'T BE A HO HO HO FOR YA BIRTHDAY!

"MY BEAUTIFUL GRANDDAUGHTER, YOUR BIRTHDAY IS NEAR,
YOU'RE GETTING SO OLD—AREN'T YOU LISTENING, DEAR?

YOU'RE SLEEPING AROUND LIKE A HO HO HO,
MEN DON'T RESPECT YOU; THEY JUST *UCK YOU AND GO!

IF YOU WANT LOVE, IT TAKES SOME TIME,
GET TO KNOW A MAN—AND, YES, ON HIS DIME!

YOU YOUNG GIRLS HATE AN OLD LADY'S ADVICE,
BUT HONEY, LET'S BE REAL—YOUR STYLE? IT'S NOT NICE.

NOW DON'T ROLL YOUR EYES; I KNOW I SOUND BOLD,
BUT ACT LIKE A LADY, AND YOU WON'T GROW OLD AND COLD!

HAPPY
Birthday

MARK

"MARK'S TALL AND CHISELED, HE'S HOT AS FIRE,
BUT BABY, HE'S JUST A WALKIN' DESIRE.

HE'LL TAKE YOU HOME, MAKE YOU SWOON AND SCREAM, BUT
HONEY, HE'S HERE FOR A ONE-NIGHT DREAM.

YOU THOUGHT HE WAS MR. RIGHT, SWEET, AND PURE? HE'S
GOT HIS UBER RUNNING, RIGHT OUT THE DOOR!"

EVAN

"Had you not jumped in on date number one,
you'd have caught all the signs and been quick to run!

He'll treat you like his next future wife,
bring you to all the important occasions in his life.

Darling, he's got ex-girlfriends on speed dial,
while he's got you thinking you'll be around for a while.

As soon as you ask for a little bit more,
your butt will be kicked right out the door."

JEFF

"JEFF'S A CHEAPSKATE, A BROKE-ASS DUDE,
MADE YOU SPLIT NACHOS, KILLED THE MOOD.

BUT DID THAT STOP YOU? OH NO, YOU STAYED BOLD,
GAVE HIM THE GRAND TOUR, LINENS AND ALL TO HOLD.

YOU THOUGHT HE WAS SWEET, A POTENTIAL BEAU,
BUT HE LEFT SMIRKING, 'GLAD I SAVED MY DOUGH!'

NEXT TIME, HONEY, SAVE THE SHEETS AND THE SASS,
FOR A GUY WHO WON'T DITCH WITH A 'THANKS FOR THE ASS!'"

HAPPY
Birthday

DAVID

"DAVID TALKS EQUALITY, WOMEN'S RIGHTS BOLD,
THEN STICKS YOU WITH THE TAB—SAYS HE'S 'NOT TRADITIONAL OR OLD.'

YOU THOUGHT, 'HE'S UNIQUE, INTERESTING, AND ODD,'
LET HIM INTO YOUR TEMPLE, ALL FOR HIS BOD.

WOMEN FOUGHT HARD FOR A BETTER WAY,
BUT NOW YOU'RE PAYING THE BILLS AND GIVING ROLLS IN THE HAY!

MAYBE HE'LL CALL, IF YOU'RE WILLING TO PAY—
TELL ME, HON, ARE WOMEN'S RIGHTS HELPING YOU TODAY?"

HAPPY
Birthday

KEVIN

"KEVIN'S A DOG THAT LIES AND CHEATS,
YOU WOULD'VE SEEN THE SIGNS IF YOU DIDN'T JUMP IN YOUR SHEETS.

HE'LL CALL YOU 'BABY,' BUT DON'T GET SOLD,
THIS MAN'S HEART, HONEY, IS ICE-COLD.

CAN'T BELIEVE YOU THOUGHT HE'D BE TRUE,
YOUR BODY IS YOUR TEMPLE, AND THIS IS THE MAN YOU GAVE IT TO!"

Henry

"Henry was a setup from a good friend,
You got all excited, thinking love was 'round the bend.

But after one night, he was gone in a flash—
No texts, no calls—just out with the trash.

You turn to your friend, furious, "What was that plan?"
She laughs, "Maybe try class next time, not a quick
bathroom slam.

Maybe if you didn't act like a whore,
He'd be back at your door, begging for more!"

LUKE

"Honey, you don't date a metro guy,
with polished nails and a well-groomed lie.

He's the kind who'll tap it, then bolt,
leaving you single as his designer coat.

Think he'd make a dad? Oh, bless—
He'll be off with others, in his skinny jeans and dress!

This pretty man—committing, oh please!
He'll be out with others, maybe them's and he's!"

HAPPY
Birthday

DAN

"DAN'S GOT A COUCH, A REMOTE, AND A PLAN—
NO NICE DINNERS, JUST 'COME OVER' DEMANDS.

HE'LL TEXT, 'COME CHILL,' WITH BEER AND TAKEOUT,
BUT HONEY, HE'LL NEVER TAKE YOU OUT AND ABOUT.

IF HE KEEPS YOU IN PRIVATE, DON'T BE A DUMMY,
HE'S JUST AFTER ONE THING—YOU MIGHT NOT FIND IT FUNNY.

NO PUBLIC DATES, NO WEEKEND BLISS,
JUST HIS 'STAY-IN SPECIAL'—NETFLIX & A QUICK... FIX!"

ALEX

"SURE, ALEX—HE'S SMOOTH, A REAL BUTTERED TREAT,
BUT HONEY, DON'T THINK YOU'RE HIS ONLY REPEAT.

IS HE PLANNING YOUR BIRTHDAY, TAKING YOU OUT?
BECAUSE THAT'S WHAT A REAL RELATIONSHIP'S ABOUT.

HE SHOULD MAKE YOU FEEL SPECIAL ON YOUR BIG DAY,
NOT JUST HIT YOU UP WHEN HE'S CRAVING A LAY."

ANDY

"YOUR BIRTHDAY'S CREEPING UP, YOU'RE FEELING THE WEIGHT,
CAN'T STAND THE THOUGHT OF A SOLO FATE!

HANDYMAN ANDY CAME TO FIX YOUR BROKEN SINK,
YOU JUMPED RIGHT ON HIM, DIDN'T EVEN THINK.

YOU'LL ADMIT, ANDY ISN'T THE BIGGEST WINNER,
BUT HEY—AT LEAST YOU DIDN'T BUY HIM DINNER!

HANDY GUYS MIGHT BE GOOD IN BED,
BUT TRUST ME, THEY'LL BOLT ONCE THEY GOT THE HEAD."

HAPPY
Birthday

TONY

"TONY'S A LATINO COWBOY, SMOOTH WITH SPICE,
BUT RIDE HIS PONY, AND YOU'LL PAY THE PRICE.

YOU HAD FUN IN THE BARN WITH NO STRINGS ATTACHED,
BUT SWEETHEART, YOUR BIRTHDAY'S COMING, AND LOVE'S NOT
MATCHED.

KEEP HORSIN' AROUND, YOU'LL END UP ALONE,
AGING AND SINGLE, JUST YOU AND YOUR PHONE!

WHEN YOUR CAKE'S GOT CANDLES, AND YOU'RE STILL WISHIN',
REMEMBER, DARLING, COMMITMENT WASN'T HIS MISSION!"

CLIFF

"CLIFF WAS A SETUP FROM YOUR BOSS,
AND, OF COURSE, YOU HAD TO GIVE IT A TOSS.

WITH YOUR BIRTHDAY LOOMING, YOU'RE FEELING THE BLUES,
HE WAS SO HANDSOME—YOU DRANK TOO MUCH BOOZE.

YOU SLEPT WITH HIM QUICK, YOU WERE IN A BIRTHDAY RUT,
NOW YOUR BOSS THINKS YOU'RE THE 'OFFICE SLUT.'

SETUPS ARE SWEET, BUT HERE'S THE THING—
THEY RARELY EVER END WITH A RING!"

HAPPY
Birthday

BILL

BILL, OH BILL, YOU MET AT THE MALL,
HADN'T BEEN THERE IN YEARS, AS YOU RECALL.

ASKED YOU FOR DINNER, NO SPLITTING THE BILL,
AND MOST IMPORTANTLY, REMEMBERED YOUR NAME IS JILL!

HE OPENS DOORS, SHOWS UP ON TIME,
MAKES YOU FEEL VALUED—A FIND SO PRIME.

NOW HERE'S THE ONE WHO'LL TREAT YOU RIGHT,
WITH HIM, YOU'LL LAUGH AND SLEEP WELL AT NIGHT.

WHEN IT'S REAL, THERE'S NO ROOM FOR DOUBT,
THIS IS THE GUY TO KEEP—NO NEED TO SWAP OUT.

HAPPY
Birthday

"NOW HONEY, MEN LOVE SEX—THAT'S AS OLD AS TIME,
BUT HANDING IT OUT FREE? WELL, THAT'S A CRIME.

BACK IN MY DAY, FAST LOVE WAS FOR PAY,
NOW GIRLS GIVE IT OUT AND GET LED ASTRAY.

WOMEN'S STANDARDS WERE HIGHER BACK WHEN I WAS TWENTY,
THEY WEREN'T PAYING FOR MEN AND GIVING AN OPEN ENTRY.

SOME MEN TURNED INTO PUSSIES, SOME EVEN WEARING DRESSES,
WHILE WOMEN GAVE UP FAMILY DREAMS, TAKING
ANTIDEPRESSANTS.

THESE DAYS, HONEY, MEN SWING BOTH WAYS WITH EASE,
ONE NIGHT IT'S YOU, NEXT NIGHT IT'S 'ANYONE HE SEES.'

HIV, STDS—DON'T BE NAÏVE,
HE'S SWAPPING PARTNERS FASTER THAN YOU'D BELIEVE!

I KNOW TIMES HAVE CHANGED, THAT'S TRUE,
BUT HOLD OUT, DEAR, FOR ONE WHO'LL LOVE YOU.
BECAUSE I DO....

HAPPY BIRTHDAY

DON'T BE A HO HO HO FOR YA BIRTHDAY!